NATURE UNFOLDS

THE POLES

BERNARD STONEHOUSE

Illustrated by

RICHARD ORR

www.crabtreebooks.com

THE POLES

THE ANTARCTIC

CONTENTS

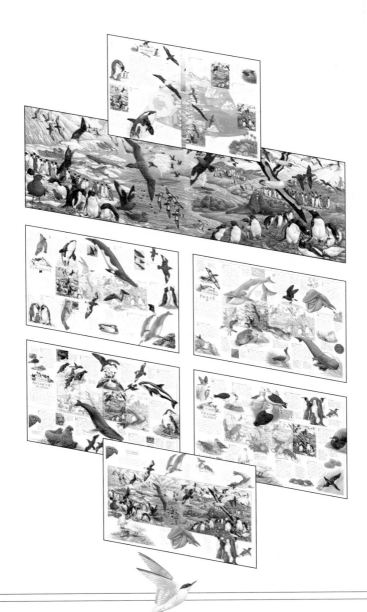

16.95

THE POLES

THE ARCTIC

CONTENTS

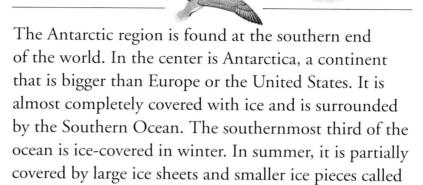

The Antarctic

The Antarctic region is found at the southern end of the world. In the center is Antarctica, a continent that is bigger than Europe or the United States. It is almost completely covered with ice and is surrounded by the Southern Ocean. The southernmost third of the ocean is ice-covered in winter. In summer, it is partially covered by large ice sheets and smaller ice pieces called **floes**. The ocean has many islands. Some are close to Antarctica, others are in warmer regions to the north. Many islands are home to wildlife, especially seabirds and seals. Antarctica is one of the world's stormiest regions.

▼ **BREEDING COLONIES**
The Southern Ocean is home to more than 60 kinds of birds. Although most of the birds come ashore to nest, these emperor penguins lay their eggs on sea ice. The penguins nest in large **colonies**, that can contain thousands of birds.

▲▼ **SEABIRDS**
Most Antarctic birds, such as the wandering albatross (below), feed by taking fish from the ocean surface. The Antarctic skua (above) catches some food at sea but also eats other birds.

◄ **CONTINENT**
Most of Antarctica is covered by a huge sheet of solid ice. This sheet can be more than 13000 feet (4000 m) high, and over 10000 feet (3000 m) thick. Underneath the ice is a smaller continent of mountains, plains, and valleys. Only a few mountains show above the ice. Much of the coast ends in tall ice cliffs. Temperatures on the ice cap rarely rise above -22° F (-30° C) and can fall below -94° F (-70° C) in winter.

Antarctic Circle

SOUTHERN OCEAN

ANTARCTICA

South Pole

Antarctic Peninsula

CHILE

ARGENTINA

Permanent pack ice

South Georgia

FULL OF FOOD ➤
Although the Southern Ocean is cold, the ocean surface is full of **phytoplankton** in summer. Phytoplankton is made of millions of tiny plant cells. These cells are food for **zooplankton**, which are tiny animals. These animals provide enough food for fishes, squid, seals, and even whales. This **orca**, or killer whale, feeds on fish, seals, and other whales.

PACK ICE ➤
Ice on the ocean surface can become 3 to 6 feet (1 to 2 m) thick in a single winter. Winds and waves break the larger ice sheets into smaller floes. These floes drift through spring and summer as **pack ice**, and gradually melt and disappear. Fish and plankton live among the floes. Seals and birds feed in the water between.

ANTARCTIC ISLANDS ➤

The islands closest to Antarctica are surrounded by sea ice in winter. In summer, the sea ice melts. The islands become warm enough for plants to grow. Many seabirds, including penguins, albatrosses, petrels, skuas, gulls, and terns, use the islands as nesting grounds.

NESTING BIRDS ➤

Most Antarctic seabirds build nests on either the Antarctic or oceanic islands. Nearly all of these birds nest in early spring, and raise their chicks during summer. There are no trees, so birds build their nests on the ground.

OCEANIC ISLANDS ▼

Oceanic islands are the farthest from the continent. These islands have warmer climates than Antarctica or the other islands. Their shorelines are covered by dense grasses and other vegetation. Large birds nest on the surface. Smaller birds dig homes into the ground called **burrows**. These burrows protect the birds from attack. Fur seals and elephant seals lie on the beaches and raise their pups close to the water's edge.

PLANT LIFE ➤

Few plants grow on Antarctica. The islands off Antarctica have milder climates and support plants such as mosses, lichens, and grasses. These islands are home to small ferns, shrubs, and flowering plants that push up through the snow in spring.

CRABEATER SEAL ▼
These seals spend winter on the pack ice. In early spring, some come to the coast to mate, or make babies. In late spring, more follow, to eat tiny **crustaceans** that live in coastal waters.

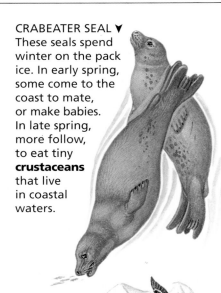

ORCA ▼

Orcas are large black-and-white mammals that swim in all the world's oceans, including the Southern Ocean. They have powerful jaws full of sharp teeth. Orcas hunt in groups among the pack ice, often close to the continent. They feed mainly on seals, fish, and penguins. Sometimes they attack and kill other whales much bigger than themselves.

Orcas have tall dorsal fins that stand up like sails. Hunting groups may include a dozen adults and three or four young whales. ▶

▼ **ANTARCTIC TERN**
These small birds have black caps and forked tail feathers that form a V-shape. Terns fly over the water and dive for small shrimp and fish.

The Antarctic

CONTINENT

Most of the Antarctic continent is covered with ice. Only parts of the coast and some mountain tops are ice-free. These are the areas in which plants can grow. The few animals that feed on land include tiny insects, **mites**, and other very small creatures that live in soil. Nearly all birds and mammals live along the Antarctic coast. They use the land for resting and breeding, but feed at sea.

▼ **EMPEROR PENGUIN**

Emperors are the largest and most colorful of all penguins. They stand over 3 feet (1 m) tall and weigh up to 100 pounds (45 kg). Females lay their eggs in autumn on sea ice. During winter, males huddle together and incubate the eggs for two months. Both parents take turns bringing food to the chicks. Their young are ready to leave the colonies in late spring.

◀ Weddell seals have large eyes for seeing in the dim light under the ice.

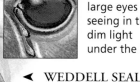

◀ **WEDDELL SEAL**

Weddell seals live under the inshore sea ice and keep their breathing holes open all winter. Mothers produce one pup in spring. When the pup is one or two weeks old, it is ready for its first swim. Weddells dive deep for fish and squid, and find food by sending out special calls that bounce off objects. This method is called **echolocation**.

▲ **ANTARCTIC PETREL**
These birds fly in flocks of several dozen. They swoop low over the water and hunt for small fish and shrimp. They nest on cliffs around the Antarctic coast.

▼ MINKE WHALE

Minke (pronounced min-key) whales are the smallest **baleen** whales. They are up to 30 feet (9 m) long. Instead of teeth, baleen whales have thin sheets of baleen, or whalebone, in their mouths. They feed by taking water into their mouths. The baleen catches small shrimp and fish, which the whales then swallow. Minkes are found all over the world. Some swim south and feed in the pack ice surrounding Antarctica.

▲ Some minkes have all-black fore-flippers (top). Most have white patches on their flippers (center and bottom).

ANTARCTIC SKUA

Antarctic skuas nest on the continent and nearby islands. They are **predators**, or hunters, and often live close to penguin colonies. Skuas feed at sea, but also eat penguin eggs and chicks that are small or dying.

ADÉLIE PENGUIN ▼

Seven **species**, or kinds, of penguins breed in the Antarctic region. Adélie penguins stand 15-20 inches (40-50 cm) tall and are the most common species on the continent. In spring, they breed in huge colonies on beaches. Both parents **incubate**, or warm, the eggs. Adélies raise their chicks during summer.

◄ Adélie penguins build nests out of pebbles that they collect from beaches.

▲ WANDERING ALBATROSS

These are the largest flying birds—their wings measure almost 13 feet (4 m) across. Albatrosses fly round the world several times each year. In summer, many fly south to feed in the waters close to Antarctica. They breed on the warmer oceanic islands.

SOUTHERN BOTTLENOSE WHALE ►

These small whales are found in deep water near Antarctica. They get their name from their rounded head, which looks like an old-fashioned bottle. In winter, the whales swim only in **polynyas**. In these areas, strong winds open up spaces between the ice. These spaces give the whales a place to come to the surface and breathe.

▼ MOSS & LICHEN

Antarctica is dry as well as cold. Often, plants such as mosses and lichens get water only when the snow melts in spring.

◄ SNOW PETREL

These small, white petrels nest high on the peaks of mountains and lay one egg at a time. They fly over the sea ice in large flocks and feed on tiny fish and plankton.

▼ PINTADO PETREL

These small petrels fly in large flocks over the sea searching for food. They land over a **shoal**, or group, of zooplankton and peck at fish and other tiny animals that they find. They nest on cliffs during summer.

The Antarctic

PACK ICE

In winter, the sea surrounding Antarctica is covered by ice floes 3 feet (1 m) or more thick. By spring, however, the floes break up and drift north. Sunlight causes tiny plant cells, or phytoplankton, in the water and ice to grow and divide. Phytoplankton is eaten by tiny floating animals, or zooplankton, as well as small fish and **krill**. These small animals provide food for seabirds, seals, and whales.

FINBACK WHALE ▼

These giant baleen whales are 80 feet (25 m) long. As with the minke (page 13) whales, their enormous mouth contains hairy-edged plates of baleen. They feed mainly on large amounts of zooplankton. Finbacks mate and produce their calves in warmer waters. In spring and summer, they bring their calves south to feed at the Antarctic pack ice.

➤ A finback's skull is 13 feet (4 m) long, and has jaws that open wide to take huge gulps of water.

➤ Big whales lift their tails out of the water to help them dive for zooplankton.

▼ ANTARCTIC FULMAR

These petrels are similar in size and shape to northern fulmars. Like most other petrels, they hunt by flying over the ocean and sea ice in flocks. Searching as a large group increases their chances of finding food. They breed in cliff colonies on Antarctica and nearby islands. If attacked, a fulmar defends itself by spitting oil from an organ near its stomach called the **crop**.

▲ DOVE PRION

Dove prions are a type of petrel. They are also called whalebirds. Prions feed in flocks and scoop up plankton from the water. There are many species of prions—each has a different beak made for eating different foods.

◀ A female prion lays a single egg in a chamber at the end of a deep burrow.

▲ NORTHERN GIANT PETREL

These large birds are similar to southern giant petrels. They breed mainly on the oceanic islands, but in summer come south to feed along the edge of the pack ice. This one is tearing into a dead seal it has found.

▼ SOUTH GEORGIA PIPIT

Unlike most Antarctic birds, this bird feeds only on land. It lives on the island of South Georgia. Like other kinds of pipits, it builds nests in grass and feeds on seeds and insects. Its main enemies are rats, which steal its eggs and chicks.

▼ GRAY-HEADED ALBATROSS

This small albatross builds a tall, circular nest of mud and grass. Each female lays a single egg in spring. The chick takes all summer and autumn to grow into an adult. These birds feed mainly on fish, squid, and plankton, which they catch at the ocean surface.

◄ Gray-headed albatrosses return to the same nest yearly. They add a few inches each year to make the nest taller.

The Antarctic

OCEANIC ISLANDS

In northern areas of the Southern Ocean, the islands are free of sea ice all year. Though some oceanic islands are covered by huge ice sheets called **glaciers**, they are warmer than islands farther south. The lowlands and coasts of these islands are green and covered with grass and shrubs. The soil is deep enough for seabirds to dig burrows, and some of the islands are home to birds that never leave the land.

SHEATHBILL ►

These birds walk like pigeons, but they are more closely related to gulls. They feed along the shore and look among seaweed for tiny snails and shrimp. They also feed in the penguin colonies, where they eat abandoned eggs, dead chicks, or food that the penguins spill on the ground.

▲ DANDELION

These weeds are common all over the world. They were brought to the southern islands accidentally by sealers and whalers.

▲ SOUTH GEORGIA PINTAIL

These little ducks are closely related to pintails in South America. In summer, they feed in freshwater ponds and streams. In winter, the ponds freeze, so pintails feed along the shores. Few nest on South Georgia today, because of the brown rats that eat their eggs.

▲ Pintails feed by **dabbling**, or searching the pond floor.

◄ **BLUE-EYED SHAG**

Shags, or cormorants, are diving birds that use both their wings and their feet to push themselves through water. Unlike penguins, they can also fly. Fish is their main food. They build their nests with seaweed and their own droppings. They lay four or five eggs, but usually raise only two or three chicks.

◄ **BROWN SKUA**
Larger than Antarctic skuas, these birds live near penguin colonies, where they steal eggs and young or weak chicks.

▼ **HOURGLASS DOLPHIN**

Dolphins are rare in Antarctic waters, but hourglass dolphins occasionally hunt near the Antarctic islands. The pattern of their white stripes varies between dolphins. Some have a black figure eight on either flank. These markings reminded early biologists of an hourglass. We know little of how these dolphins live or what they feed on.

▲ Shags swim with their wings out and push with their feet.

CHINSTRAP PENGUIN ▼

Chinstraps are closely related to Adélie penguins but are slightly smaller. They are recognizable by the narrow band of black feathers under their chin. They breed in large colonies of over 10000 birds. When entering the sea to wash or hunt, they keep together in groups. These groups make it harder for leopard seals and other predators to catch them.

▼ The bumps on the humpback's face may contain organs that help them find food.

▲ **LEOPARD SEAL**

Leopard seals have spotted coats and strong jaws. These seals live alone and feed mainly among the pack ice. Some hunt near penguin colonies on the Antarctic islands. As penguins approach the shore, the seal kills one with a bite. It then shakes off the bird's feathery skin before swallowing the body.

▲ A fur seal's soft underfur is covered by long guard hairs.

▼ **SOUTHERN FUR SEAL**
Fur seals have a kind of fur that was made into valuable coats. In the early 1800s, they were hunted until there were few left. Now there are more of them again. Females give birth to a single black pup.

◄ **SOOTY SHEARWATER**
Sooty shearwaters nest on islands near places like Australia. In summer, flocks of one-year-old birds fly south to feed on Antarctic plankton.

▼ A gull parent brings up food from its crop when chicks tap its beak.

▼ DOMINICAN GULL

These large gulls nest on the southern islands, as well as the Antarctic Peninsula. They search beaches and shallow waters for food, and eat plankton and small fish. Their chicks are covered by brown speckles that help them blend into their background. This blending is called **camouflage**.

◄ In the 1700s, "macaroni" was a name for elegant men who wore colored feathers in their hats.

▼ MACARONI PENGUIN

From the neck down macaronis look like many other penguins. On their forehead, however, are two crests of golden-yellow feathers. They shake these feathers during the mating season to attract partners. Macaronis nest in big colonies, mainly on Antarctic and oceanic islands. They lay two eggs, one larger than the other. Parents usually raise only the one chick from the larger egg.

◄ Macaroni penguins sometimes have to scramble up slippery slopes to reach their nests.

The Antarctic

ANTARCTIC ISLANDS

The oceanic islands closest to Antarctica are surrounded by pack ice for over half the year. They are almost as cold as nearby continental coasts in winter, but they become warmer in summer. After the snow has disappeared, the beaches and cliffs become greener. These islands share many species of plants, birds, and seals with Antarctica. More-northern islands outside the pack-ice zone are even warmer throughout the year.

ELEPHANT SEAL

These seals get their name from the male's trunk-like nose. This nose develops at the start of the breeding season. The trunk looks fierce and is used to frighten off other males. While fighting for space in the crowded breeding colonies, males rise up and bash each other with their chest and head. Pups have to be alert to avoid being squashed. ➤

◄ Female elephant seals have a normal nose. Their whiskers help them find food in the dark.

➤ HUMPBACK WHALE

Humpbacks are named for the small hump in the middle of their back, which shows above the water when they dive. These whales are up to 56 feet (17 m) in length, and have long, narrow flippers. Mothers give birth to their young in warmer waters. They then bring their calves south to feed on Antarctic zooplankton.

▲ When fighting, male elephant seals can scar each other with their teeth. These cuts are usually not serious.

STORM PETREL ▼

Wilson's storm petrels and black-bellied storm petrels are two closely related species. These birds rarely land on the water, but instead float and peck for tiny animals in the spaces between ice floes. They nest in deep crevices among rocks, and raise one chick at a time.

PHYTOPLANKTON ➤

Phytoplankton is made of thousands of tiny green cells. Each cell collects nutrients from water and energy from sunlight. These ingredients combine to produce more cells. By early summer there is enough phytoplankton to color the sea cloudy green.

▼ BLUE WHALE

Blue whales are the largest animals on Earth and are 105 feet (32 m) long. They are baleen whales and use their mouths to filter zooplankton from the sea. Blue whales give birth to their calves in warmer seas, and migrate to the Southern Ocean for the summer months. They often swim close to the northern edge of the pack ice.

▼ SOUTHERN GIANT PETREL

Giant petrels catch fish and squid at sea, but they also hunt on land. They attack penguins and scavenge **carcasses** of seals and whales. There are two closely related species of giant petrels. The southern species breeds on the colder Antarctic islands.

▲ Giant petrels have strong beaks, which they use to tear flesh from dead penguins and seals.

▲ ROSS SEAL

Ross seals live mostly on the pack ice. They dive into deep water to eat squid. Ross seals mate in water. They come up on the pack ice mainly to rest and give birth to pups.

➤ SPERM WHALE

Unlike baleen whales, sperms are toothed whales. They have a narrow lower jaw with 20 or more teeth. They feed mainly on giant squid, for which they dive as deep as 3300 feet (1000 m). Although sperm whales spend most of their lives in warm seas, adult males visit Antarctic waters in summer.

◄ LIGHT-MANTLED SOOTY ALBATROSS

Most albatrosses are white, but these birds are gray-brown. They are smaller than wandering albatrosses, and nest on the oceanic islands. They fly south in summer to feed in the pack ice.

➤ ZOOPLANKTON

Zooplankton feeds on phytoplankton and is made up of many kinds of small animals. These include **larval**, or young, starfish, worms, and crabs.

◄ BLACK-BROWED ALBATROSS

These birds are similar in appearance to gray-headed albatrosses, but they have dark gray feathers above their eyes. They nest on cliffs and slopes of the Southern Ocean islands. Albatrosses build their nest where strong winds blow. These winds make it easier for them to take off from the nest and soar above the cliffs.

◄ Courting albatrosses get to know each other by **billing**, or crossing their bills, and calling.

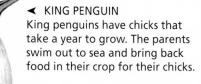

◄ KING PENGUIN

King penguins have chicks that take a year to grow. The parents swim out to sea and bring back food in their crop for their chicks.

◄ A chick sits on its parent's feet for warmth.

WHITE-CHINNED PETREL ▼

White-chinned petrels fly in flocks over the ocean. They land to make shallow dives for squid, shrimp, and fish. These petrels nest in burrows up to six and a half feet (2 m) long, which they dig with their beaks and webbed feet.

TUSSOCK GRASS ▼

This tough grass grows in large clumps on the shores of many of the oceanic islands. Pipits eat its seeds and some petrels nest among its roots. Fur seals rest on top of clumps of tussock grass.

BROWN RAT ▲

When whaling ships first landed on the oceanic islands, brown rats from the ships began living there. Today, the rats survive close to the shore. In winter they live under the snow, nesting and feeding among tussock grass roots. They may also feed on small birds and their eggs. This feeding has driven some birds away from the larger islands.

▼ MOSS CUSHION
On warmer islands, some mosses grow into round cushions about 3 feet (1 m) across. The cushions are big enough for birds to burrow and nest under.

GENTOO PENGUIN

Gentoos breed all over the Antarctic region—from the cold Antarctic Peninsula to the warmer northern islands. They build nests out of stones and raise two gray-and-white chicks. At sea, they catch small fish and shrimp. They hunt mainly in surface waters, but can dive to depths of 100 feet (30 m) or more. ►

The Antarctic

KEY TO FOLD-OUT

Use these key numbers if you want to identify any of the animals and plants on the Antarctic fold-out. You can read about them on pages 12-19, where they are all featured.

Elephant Seal (34)

Southern Bottlenose Whale (9)

Antarctic Petrel (1)

1 Antarctic Petrel
2 Snow Petrel
3 Weddell Seal
4 Emperor Penguin
5 Antarctic Skua
6 Lichens
7 Moss
8 Adélie Penguin

Sheathbill (50)

9 Southern Bottlenose Whale
10 Wandering Albatross
11 Orca or Killer Whale
12 Crabeater Seal
13 Antarctic Tern
14 Minke Whale
15 Ross Seal
16 Antarctic Fulmar
17 Northern Giant Petrel
18 Dove Prion

The Arctic

The Arctic is the northernmost end of the world. It extends from the North Pole to the **tree line,** which is the northern limit of forests. It includes the Arctic Ocean, Greenland, and northern parts of Alaska, Canada, Scandinavia, and Siberia. Arctic lands are snow-covered in winter. But there are large areas where mosses, lichens, grasses, and other small plants grow. Many insects, birds, and mammals feed among the plants.

► MOSSES AND LICHENS
Mosses, lichens, and algae live on the tundra and the polar desert. Here there is moisture and shelter from strong winds.

► GRAZING MAMMALS
Few grazing mammals live in the Arctic. These white Dall's sheep go hungry in winter, but feed well when the snow disappears in spring.

► THE TUNDRA
In warmer areas, winters are shorter and summers longer. Snow covers the ground for eight or nine months each year, but melts in summer. There is usually enough snow and rain to keep the ground moist. This moisture gives the tundra richer vegetation than the polar desert. This vegetation provides more food for the animals living there.

► Geese fly long distances from **temperate,** or warm, areas to feed in the Arctic every summer.

► POLAR DESERT
In the far north, winters are long and cold, and summers are short. There is little snow or rain, so the ground is dry. To avoid strong winds, plants that grow there are low to the ground . A few birds, mammals, and insects live there.

◄ FLOWERING PLANTS
Many flowering plants bloom in the tundra in early summer, including these pink saxifrages and Arctic poppies. Insects feed on a sweet liquid in the flowers called **nectar.**

Brown Rat (41)

Leopard Seal (32)

19 Southern Giant Petrel
20 Sperm Whale
21 Light-Mantled Sooty Albatross
22 Finback Whale
23 Zooplankton
24 Pintado Petrel
25 Phytoplankton
26 Storm Petrel
27 Blue Whale

28 Hourglass Dolphin
29 Brown Skua
30 Humpback Whale
31 Southern Fur Seal
32 Leopard Seal

43 Moss Cushion
44 Gentoo Penguin
45 King Penguin
46 White-Chinned Petrel
47 Dandelion
48 South Georgia Pintail
49 Tussock Grass
50 Sheathbill

Blue Whale (27)

33 Macaroni Penguin
34 Elephant Seal
35 Blue-Eyed Shag
36 Chinstrap Penguin
37 Dominican Gull
38 Sooty Shearwater
39 Black-Browed Albatross
40 Gray-Headed Albatross
41 Brown Rat
42 South Georgia Pipit

King Penguin (45)

DALL'S SHEEP ▶

These tough mountain sheep live in the Rocky Mountains. **Rams**, or males, have large curling horns. **Ewes**, or females, have smaller horns. The horns grow throughout life. In spring, rams fight each other for mates and territory.

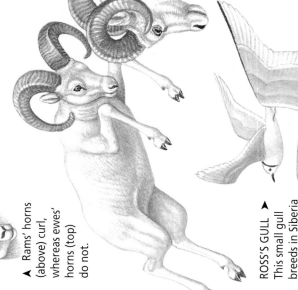

▲ Rams' horns (above) curl, whereas ewes' horns (top) do not.

ROSS'S GULL ▶

This small gull breeds in Siberia and Greenland. It lives mostly on land, and feeds on insects. Ross's gull rarely flies far from the Arctic.

▶ MUSK OX

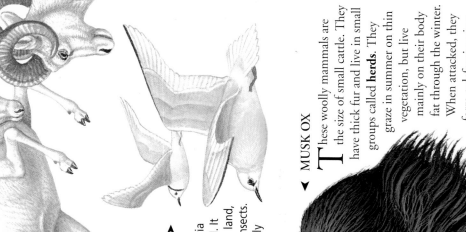

These woolly mammals are the size of small cattle. They have thick fur and live in small groups called **herds**. They graze in summer on thin vegetation, but live mainly on their body fat through the winter. When attacked, they form a defensive ring and stand with horns pointing outward. Their calves hide inside the circle.

The Arctic

POLAR DESERT

The coldest parts of the Arctic are very dry. The soil is thin and full of gravel, and can be blown away by strong winds. Snow that falls in winter disappears quickly in spring and leaves behind little water for plants or animals. Without good soil or moisture, few plants can grow. Only the toughest plants can survive in sheltered corners of the desert.

BARNACLE GOOSE ▶

These geese spend winter in northern Europe. In spring they fly north to Arctic islands to raise their young. Mothers pluck soft feathers called **down** from their body to keep their eggs warm.

▶ Unlike most geese, barnacle geese often nest on cliffs and ledges. Here, the geese and their chicks are safer from foxes and other predators.

BEWICK'S SWAN ▶

In winter, Bewick's swans live in warm areas. In spring, they migrate north to build nests on the tundra. Their long necks reach deep into the water, where they feed on pond weeds. They raise four or five **cygnets**, or young, which fly south with them in autumn.

▲ Swans have unique facial markings. People who study them often recognize them individually.

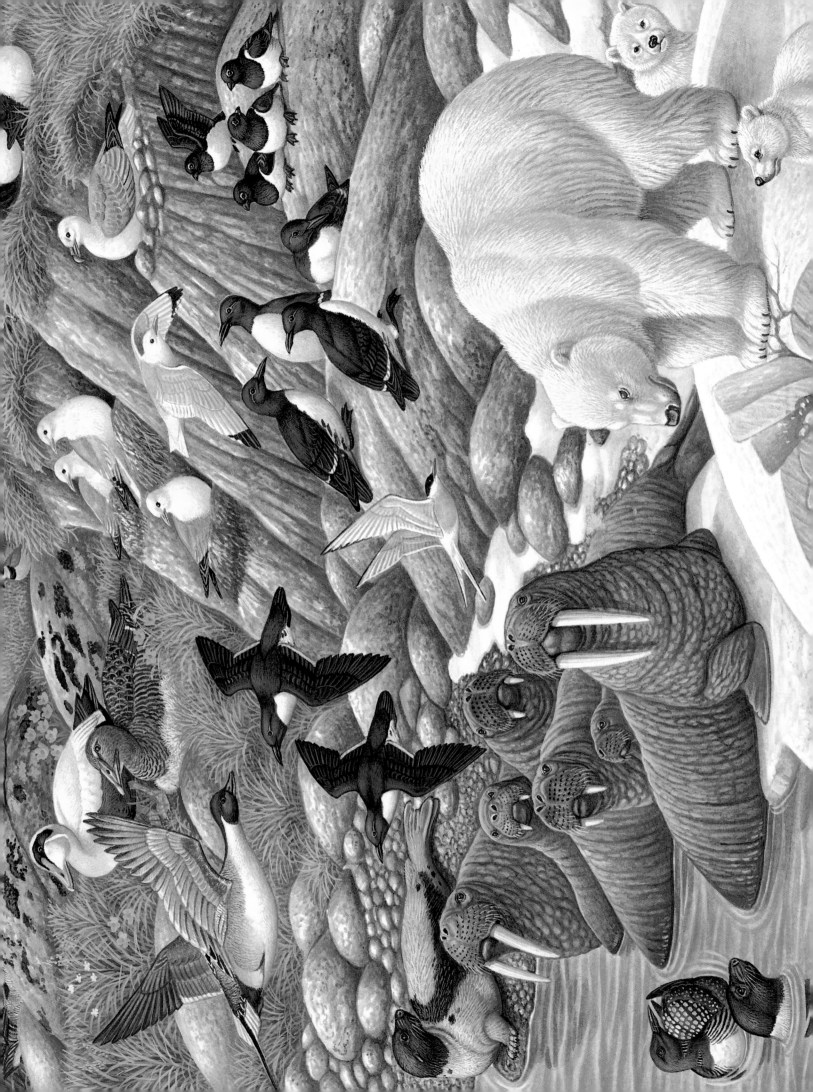

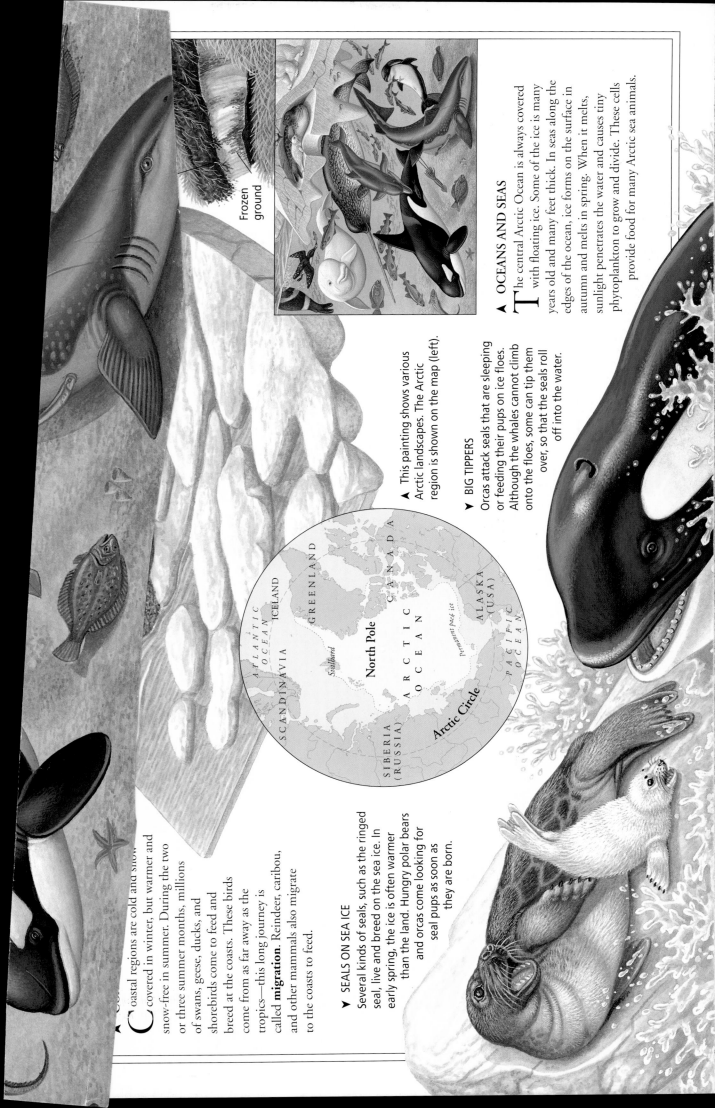

Coastal regions are cold and snow covered in winter, but warmer and snow-free in summer. During the two or three summer months, millions of swans, geese, ducks, and shorebirds come to feed and breed at the coasts. These birds come from as far away as the tropics—this long journey is called **migration**. Reindeer, caribou, and other mammals also migrate to the coasts to feed.

Frozen ground

▼ SEALS ON SEA ICE
Several kinds of seals, such as the ringed seal, live and breed on the sea ice. In early spring, the ice is often warmer than the land. Hungry polar bears and orcas come looking for seal pups as soon as they are born.

▲ OCEANS AND SEAS
The central Arctic Ocean is always covered with floating ice. Some of the ice is many years old and many feet thick. In seas along the edges of the ocean, ice forms on the surface in autumn and melts in spring. When it melts, sunlight penetrates the water and causes tiny phytoplankton to grow and divide. These cells provide food for many Arctic sea animals.

▲ This painting shows various Arctic landscapes. The Arctic region is shown on the map (left).

▶ BIG TIPPERS
Orcas attack seals that are sleeping or feeding their pups on ice floes. Although the whales cannot climb onto the floes, some can tip them over, so that the seals roll off into the water.

Map labels:
ATLANTIC OCEAN
ICELAND
GREENLAND
SCANDINAVIA
Svalbard
North Pole
ARCTIC OCEAN
CANADA
SIBERIA (RUSSIA)
Permanent pack ice
ALASKA (USA)
PACIFIC OCEAN
Arctic Circle

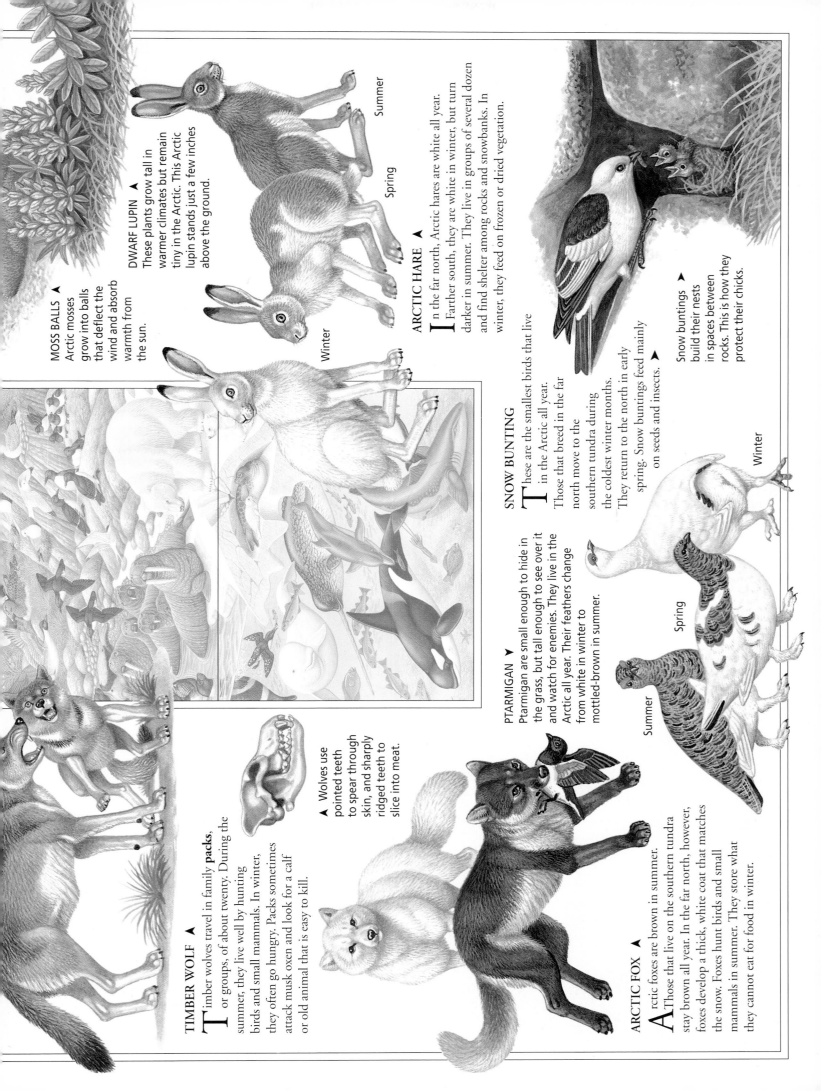

MOSS BALLS ▲
Arctic mosses grow into balls that deflect the wind and absorb warmth from the sun.

DWARF LUPIN ▲
These plants grow tall in warmer climates but remain tiny in the Arctic. This Arctic lupin stands just a few inches above the ground.

Summer

Spring

Winter

ARCTIC HARE ▲

I n the far north, Arctic hares are white all year. Farther south, they are white in winter, but turn darker in summer. They live in groups of several dozen and find shelter among rocks and snowbanks. In winter, they feed on frozen or dried vegetation.

SNOW BUNTING

T hese are the smallest birds that live in the Arctic all year. Those that breed in the far north move to the southern tundra during the coldest winter months. They return to the north in early spring. Snow buntings feed mainly on seeds and insects. ▲

Snow buntings ▲
build their nests in spaces between rocks. This is how they protect their chicks.

PTARMIGAN ▶
Ptarmigan are small enough to hide in the grass, but tall enough to see over it and watch for enemies. They live in the Arctic all year. Their feathers change from white in winter to mottled-brown in summer.

Winter

Spring

Summer

TIMBER WOLF ▲

T imber wolves travel in family **packs**, or groups, of about twenty. During the summer, they live well by hunting birds and small mammals. In winter, they often go hungry. Packs sometimes attack musk oxen and look for a calf or old animal that is easy to kill.

▲ Wolves use pointed teeth to spear through skin, and sharply ridged teeth to slice into meat.

ARCTIC FOX ▲

A rctic foxes are brown in summer. Those that live on the southern tundra stay brown all year. In the far north, however, foxes develop a thick, white coat that matches the snow. Foxes hunt birds and small mammals in summer. They store what they cannot eat for food in winter.

The Arctic

THE TUNDRA

The tundra is warmer in summer than the polar desert. It has deeper soils and more moisture to support more plants and animals. The richest tundra soil is found in coastal lowlands, and in moist ground close to river banks along the northern tree line. Grazing mammals and feeding birds leave droppings on the ground, which help keep the soil full of minerals.

RUFF AND REEVE ▶
Ruffs are male birds with a reddish-brown **ruff**, or collar, of feathers. Females are called reeves, but have no collar. The ruffs display their collars to attract a reeve.

◀ CARIBOU
North American caribou are similar to the reindeer of Europe and Asia. Unlike reindeer, caribou live wild. Caribou spend winter in the forests. In spring, they move in enormous herds onto the tundra to eat grasses and lichens. Males grow large branched antlers, which they **shed**, or lose, each year. Females have smaller antlers, which they use to clear the snow from their food.

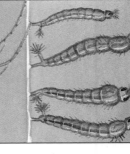
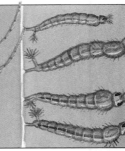

MOSQUITO ▶
Mosquito eggs survive winter in ponds and lakes. They appear in early spring as larvae (bottom right), and feed on tiny plants in the water. The larvae then become adult mosquitoes (top right), which live for a few days, mate, and lay eggs. Female mosquitoes feed by sucking blood from birds or mammals.

BLACK-TAILED GODWIT ▶
About 30 species of shorebirds fly north in spring to the Arctic tundra. The brown speckles of these godwits provide camouflage against the grasses and shrubs of their nests.

CANADA GOOSE ▶
These geese live in different places, but many fly north in spring to nest on the tundra. They lay six or seven eggs, and both parents guard the nest. When the eggs hatch, parents and chicks feed on the lakes, where they can be safe from land predators.

◀ BUTTERFLY
Several species of butterfly breed in warmer parts of the tundra. Their eggs survive the winter, and caterpillars emerge in spring to feed on fresh leaves. Many caterpillars are eaten by birds, or die of cold during spring frosts. Arctic butterflies are usually paler than southern species.

Arctic foxes eat the eggs of snow geese

to breed in the Arctic. When approached by a predator, the plover staggers as though it has a broken wing. This act is done to draw attention away from its chicks.

▶ A grizzly's huge front paw has five fingers, each armed with a sharp claw.

GRIZZLY BEAR ▶

Grizzly (meaning gray) is the name given to the big brown bears of Alaska and northwestern Canada that have long gray hairs in their coats. Grizzlies eat a wide variety of foods, including berries, leaves, eggs, small mammals, and salmon that they catch in streams.

PIKA ▶

These small mammals live among rocks high in the mountains. They feed on vegetation. Pika pack their burrows with dried grass and leaves to keep them warm through the winter.

WOLVERINE ▶

These fierce predators are related to otters and badgers, and have powerful jaws. Wolverines live mainly in forests, but often hunt on the tundra as well. In spring, females produce two or three cubs, which hunt along with them throughout the summer.

A wolverine can kill animals much larger than itself, such as a caribou. ▶

SNOW GOOSE ▲

This name is given to several species of white geese that fly north to breed on the Arctic tundra. They have black wingtips and orange-pink legs and beaks. Sometimes, they arrive at the nesting places while snow is still on the ground. They have to wait two or three weeks before they can start to build their nests.

BALD EAGLE ▶

These white-headed birds live in the wilderness of Alaska. Here they are safe from shooting or poisoning by people. They nest in tall trees and cliffs that overlook the sea. From these spots, they can watch for fish and other **prey**, or animals to hunt. ▶

BEARBERRY ▲

When the snow has gone, these shrubs grow in groups on the tundra. In summer they produce flowers, which turn into clusters of bright berries by autumn. Bearberries get their name because bears eat them.

PUFFIN ▶

Puffins are sometimes called "sea parrots." They are found only in the north Atlantic and nearby parts of the Arctic Ocean. Puffins nest by burrowing in grassy spots on cliff-tops, usually right by the sea. They eat small fish, which they catch by diving.

▲ Young puffins in their first year have a gray face and reddish bill.

◀ RINGED PLOVER

These small shorebirds breed on the coastal tundra in summer. They feed on insects and seeds. Plovers lay three or four eggs in a simple nest on the ground. They are called ringed plovers because of the band of dark feathers across their breast.

▶ Despite their size, even walruses are not safe from attack by polar bears.

The Arctic

COASTLANDS

The Arctic coastlands and sea ice near shore provide homes for land and sea animals. Many seabirds, some ducks, walruses, and seals feed at sea. These animals come ashore or onto the coastal ice to rest and breed. Polar bears wander freely between land and ice, using both for hunting and resting.

COMMON EIDER ▶

These ducks live close to the sea. They feed in rock pools or in shallow waters just offshore. Females have mottled brown camouflage to protect them when they are on the nest. They sit still to avoid being seen by predators.

▶ Eiders line their nests with soft down. Hunters collect it and sell it as eiderdown.

BUTTERCUP ▶

Many kinds of garden plants have close relatives that live in the Arctic. For example, several different kinds of buttercups grow in different parts of the tundra and along the coast. They grow low to the ground to avoid strong winds.

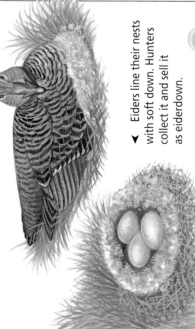

KITTIWAKE ▶

Kittiwakes nest on cliffs overlooking patches of the sea. They choose spots near areas where the sea ice clears early. They compete noisily with one another for the narrow nesting ledges. The birds' name comes from their noisy calls.

WALRUS

Male walruses measure over 13 feet (4 m) and are one of the largest seals. Females are smaller, and less than half the weight of males. Walruses live close to the coast of the Arctic and other oceans. They feed by diving to the muddy sea floor and searching for clams and other shellfish. Their tusks are used to scrape food from the mud.

▲ Walruses are hunted for their big tusks, which can be carved like elephant ivory.

DOVEKIE
Dovekies are tiny seabirds. They use their wings not only for flying, but also for swimming. They hunt by diving through the waves and catching tiny fish and shrimp in their beaks. They nest in large colonies on the cliffs of Arctic islands.

MEADOW VOLE ▲
Voles are mouse-like rodents with small ears and tails that are about half their body length. Meadow voles live in warmer areas of the tundra. They feed on insects, plants, and seeds. They live among grasses in summer and burrow under the snow in winter.

RIBBON SEAL ▶

These seals have a brown coat with white or creamy-yellow ribbons.

They live only in the northern Pacific Ocean, from Japan in the east to Alaska in the west. Their usual habitat is on pack ice far from land. They give birth to a single white pup in early spring.

When they are underwater, seals close their nostrils to keep the water out. ▶

GREAT NORTHERN DIVER

Divers breed inland close to lakes, but often feed along the ocean coast. They show only their heads and tops of their backs when swimming. They can dive over 200 feet (60 m) in search of food.

POLAR BEAR ▶

These large white bears spend half their lives at sea. They search the ice for seals, which are their main prey. Their white fur is not only thick, it has hollow hairs which allow the sun's heat to penetrate and warm their skin. On land they eat almost any plant or animal that they find. Mothers give birth to two or three cubs in snowbank dens during winter. The family comes out to search for food in spring.

HARP SEAL ▲
These seals have a harp-shaped brown patch on their backs. Harp seal pups are born white. In winter, they live on the Arctic pack ice, where they are safe from killer whales.

The Arctic

OCEANS AND SEAS

Much of the Arctic Ocean is permanently covered in ice. The shallow seas around it are home to many animals. The seas are covered by ice in winter but they are full of **plankton** in summer. Larger animals come to these seas to eat this plankton. For centuries, humans have hunted these seas for whales, seals, fish, shrimp, and seabirds.

RINGED SEAL ▶

These small seals have dark gray blotches, ringed with white. They live on inshore ice and eat fish and plankton. Females find shelter among the ice floes where they give birth to their pups in March and April.

◀ BELUGA

Beluga is Russian for "white." These whales grow up to 16 feet (5 m) long, and live in groups of about 20. Sometimes, bigger herds of several hundred whales are formed. Beluga calves are born in July, and can immediately swim with the rest of the herd.

▲ Whale calves are born tail-first and are pushed to the surface for their first breath.

SHRIMP ▶

At one time, Arctic shrimp and prawns were eaten only by fish, seals, and other natural predators. In recent years, fishermen have used giant nets to catch them for food.

SAITHE ▶

Saithe are silvery-gray fish that live in big shoals in Arctic seas. They feed on small cod, but are eaten by larger cod, seals, and whales. Saithe are caught by fishers for market.

▶ A saithe hunts small cod, which are its main prey.

COD ▶

Arctic cod live in Arctic seas. They feed near the sea floor on smaller fish, crabs, and sea urchins. Cod migrate every year to certain areas to lay their eggs on the sea floor. Arctic fishers know these areas and catch the cod.

▲ Cods' eggs laid on the sea floor float to the surface and turn into larvae. Soon they become small fish that feed on the plankton.

NARWHAL ▶

These silvery-gray whales have a spiraled tusk in front of their head, which may grow over 6 feet (2 m) long. Males always have one, females sometimes do. Scientists do not know how narwhals use them, but they may be for fighting. The tusks were once used by people to make walking-sticks, lamp-stands, and bedposts.

▲ This orca is biting a harp seal with its strong teeth.

▲ ORCA

Orcas move through the sea in family groups. Each group has several males, females, and calves. Orcas swim into Arctic waters in summer. Big males have tall dorsal fins that stand six and a half feet (2 m) high on their backs.

▲ HERRING

Herring form large **shoals** in Arctic seas. Their eggs are laid near the surface but fall to the sea floor to hatch. Herring feed almost entirely on phytoplankton and zooplankton. They use strainers on their gills to filter the food out of the water.

▶ LAMPREY
This small fish (circled) attaches itself to larger fish and feeds on their flesh.

▲ Lampreys use their circular rows of teeth for a firm grip.

▲ GREENLAND SHARK

Most sharks live in warm waters, but Greenland sharks live in cold waters of the north Atlantic Ocean. They grow 21 feet (6.5 m) long. They live and feed deep in the ocean, but sometimes come to the surface.

PLAICE ▶

Plant and animal debris of all kinds falls through the water and settles on the sea floor. Starfish, worms, crabs, and many other animals eat this debris. These animals are eaten by "flatfish," such as plaice and halibut, whose shapes allow them to lie flat on the sea floor.

▶ Plaice can change their skin color to hide on the sea floor.

▶ The tusk is made of two teeth in the upper jaw that grow forward and twist around each other.

▶ GRENADIER

These fish live in Arctic seas as deep as 1300 feet (400 m) or deeper. They feed mainly on the sea floor, and are hunted by seals. Fishermen catch them for market.

STARFISH ▶
Starfish crawl over the sea floor and feed on debris and small animals. This one has caught a mussel. It uses its many suckers to pull open the shell and eat the flesh inside.

▶ If a starfish has an arm bitten off, it can regrow it.

The Arctic

KEY TO FOLD-OUT

Use these key numbers if you want to identify any of the animals and plants on the Arctic fold-out. Most of them are featured on pages 28–35, and are listed here in bold type.

Those that are not featured are also listed with a brief description.

1 **Dall's Sheep**
2 **Bewick's Swan**
3 **Barnacle Goose**
4 **Ross's Gull**
5 **Musk Ox**
6 **Moss Balls**
7 **Timber Wolf**
8 Snowy Owl
These large black-and-white speckled owls hunt in the tundra during the day for lemmings and small birds.
9 **Arctic Hare**
10 **Arctic Fox**
11 Icelandic Gull
Icelandic gulls breed on rocky cliffs in Greenland, but winter on the coasts of Iceland and northern Britain.
12 **Ptarmigan**
13 Lichens
These small plants are made of algae and fungi. They can be gray, red, yellow, orange, or black. Lichens live in cold, dry areas and grow on rocks or other plants.
14 **Snow Bunting**

36 Bumblebee
About a dozen species of these bees live and breed in the Arctic. They spread pollen between flowers in summer.
37 Forget-me-not
These tiny plants with sky-blue flowers grow wild on the Arctic tundra.
38 Lemming
Several kinds of these rodents live on the tundra in underground burrows.
39 **Puffin**
40 **Meadow Vole**
41 **Ringed Plover**
42 **Buttercup**
43 Green-Winged Teal
These small ducks breed in Arctic North America, and fly south to the southern United States in winter.
44 Pintail
These birds have long necks and tails that are different from other Arctic ducks.
45 **Common Eider**
46 **Kittiwake**
47 Northern Fulmar
These birds nest on cliffs, where they are safe from predators.
48 **Dovekie**
49 Bridled Guillemot
Although they stand and swim like penguins, they can fly as well.
50 Arctic Tern
Arctic terns breed in the far north and in winter fly the length of the world to the Southern Ocean.

Puffin (39)

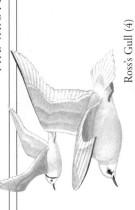

Ross's Gull (4)

Arctic Fox (10)

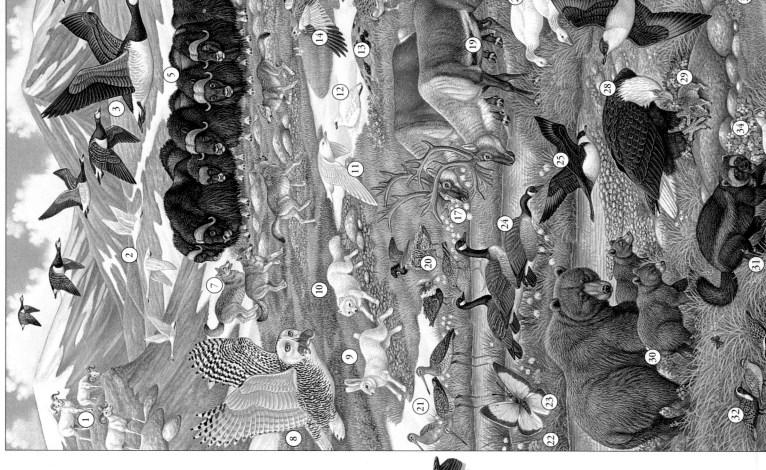

Grizzly Bear (30)

51 **Common Guillemot**
The wings of these seabirds are excellent for swimming.

52 **Harp Seal**
53 **Great Northern Diver**
54 **Ribbon Seal**
55 **Walrus**
56 **Polar Bear**
57 **Ringed Seal**
58 **Saithe**
59 **Beluga**
60 **Redfish**
This species lives in deep water far from land. Redfish are hunted by hooded seals.

61 **Narwhal**
62 **Bottlenosed Dolphin**
These warm water dolphins sometimes follow shoals of fish into colder Arctic waters.

63 **Herring**
64 **Shrimp**
65 **Mackerel**
These fish are hunted by both marine mammals and people.

66 **Common Porpoise**
These small porpoises live in groups of ten to twenty, and are found in coastal seas of the north Atlantic Ocean.

67 **Plaice**
68 **Greenland Shark**
69 **Lamprey**
70 **Squid**
Squid are close relatives of the octopus. They live in all the world's oceans, and catch food with their long tentacles.

71 **Orca**
72 **Cod**
73 **Grenadier**
74 **Starfish**
75 **Halibut**
Like plaice, halibut have flat bodies for lying on the sea floor. They are spotted to blend into their background.

Starfish (74)

Ribbon Seal (54)

15 **Dwarf Rhododendron**
When this Arctic flower is fully grown, it is less than one foot (30 cm) high.

16 **Dwarf Lupin**
17 **Cotton Grass**
Arctic cotton grass grows in damp areas of the tundra, such as near ponds and streams.

18 **Mosquito**
19 **Caribou**
20 **Ruff**
21 **Black-tailed Godwit**
22 **Marsh Fleabane**
Several kinds of this flower grow on the tundra.

23 **Butterfly**
24 **Canada Goose**
25 **Pomarine Skua**
These skuas breed in the Arctic, and catch voles, mice, and insects to feed their chicks.

26 **Snow Goose**
27 **Arctic Skua**
Arctic skuas catch other birds, voles, and mice.

28 **Bald Eagle**
29 **Pika**
30 **Grizzly Bear**
31 **Wolverine**
32 **American Golden Plover**
33 **Ermine**
These small weasels are about one foot (30 cm) long. They are dark brown in summer, but turn white in winter.

Bearberry (34)

34 **Bearberry**
35 **Saxifrage**
On the tundra, seven or eight species of this plant grow wild and flower throughout summer.

THE POLES

—— GLOSSARY ——

alga (*plural* **algae**) A plant, usually green or red in color, that has a simple cell structure

Antarctic Circle An imaginary circle on Earth's surface, south of which there is at least one day each year in which the sun does not rise above the horizon

Arctic Circle An imaginary circle on Earth's surface, north of which there is at least one day each year in which the sun does not rise above the horizon

baleen Thin, stiff material that hangs in the mouth of some whales and is used to filter food out of water

breathing hole A hole in the ice through which a seal can breathe

breeding colony A group of birds or other animals breeding together

camouflage A color pattern on an animal that allows it to hide from enemies

carcass The body of a dead animal

caterpillar The larva of a butterfly

cell The smallest living unit of a plant or animal

colony A place occupied by a group of animals of the same kind

crop The pouch-like first stomach of a bird, in which it can store food to feed its young

crustacean Sea animals, such as crabs and shrimp, that have a hard outer skeleton but no backbone

dorsal fin The fin along the back of a fish or whale

echolocation An animal's ability to find its way around and locate food by sending and receiving sounds

fungus (*plural* **fungi**) A living thing, such as mushrooms or mold, which gets its food from both living and dead things

gill The breathing organ of a fish

glacier A slow-moving stream of ice

guard hair Long hair that protects an animal's underfur and keeps its skin dry

habitat The natural place where a plant or animal is found

ice cap One of two masses of ice that cover the Arctic region and Antarctica

ice floe A fragment of floating sea ice, usually one that has broken off of a larger sheet

incubate When an animal keeps its eggs warm until they are ready to hatch by covering them with its body

ivory The hard, bony material that makes up teeth and tusks

krill A tiny crustacean that is eaten in large amounts by baleen whales

larva (*plural* **larvae**) The young form of an animal, which is different from its adult form

lichen A plant made up of algae and fungi

migrate To move from one location to another in order to mate or find food or water

mineral A natural non-living earth substance

mite A tiny animal, related to spiders, which often lives on animals or plants

moss A green plant with small simple leaves, non-woody stems, and no roots

nectar A sugary liquid produced by plants to attract insects

North Pole The northern end of the axis of Earth's rotation, from which all directions lead south

pack ice A mass of large blocks of ice formed by ice floes being forced together

phytoplankton Tiny, free-floating plants found at the surface of a sea or lake

plankton Floating organisms, such as algae, found in a body of water

polar desert A dry area in a polar region where there is little rain or snow and few plants grow

pollen Powder produced by flowers to fertilize other flowers

polynya A patch of unfrozen sea surrounded by sea ice

predator An animal that kills and eats other animals

prey An animal that is hunted by another animal

scavenge To hunt for dead animals and similar foods

shoal (*also called* school) A group of fish or other sea animals

South Pole The southern end of the axis of Earth's rotation, from which all directions lead north

spawn To release eggs

species A group of similar living things whose offspring can reproduce

thaw To melt, especially ice

tree line The furthest northern point that trees grow

zooplankton Tiny, free-floating animals found at the surface of a sea or lake